THE
POWER
OF
GOD

THE POWER OF GOD

Craig W. Hagin

FAITH LIBRARY PUBLICATIONS

Unless otherwise indicated, all Scripture quotations in this volume are from the *King James Version* of the Bible.

First Edition
Second Printing 1999

ISBN 0-89276-900-9

In the U.S. write:
Kenneth Hagin Ministries
P.O. Box 50126
Tulsa, OK 74150-0126

In Canada write:
Kenneth Hagin Ministries
P.O. Box 335, Station D
Etobicoke (Toronto), Ontario
Canada, M9A 4X3

Contents

Chapter 1
Put Your Faith in the Power of God

No matter what you're going through right now, God's power is greater than the circumstance. Think about God and how good He has been to you. Remember all the times that He has delivered you from problems in the past. Well, God is *still* in the delivering business. When you know His power, who He is, and what He's done, you can't help but be excited!

It's important that you understand how mighty the power of God is. His power created the heavens and the earth and everything in the earth. The power of God *cannot* and *will not* fail you! That's the kind of power you need to put your faith in!

1 CORINTHIANS 2:1-5
1 And I, brethren, when I came to you, came not with

excellency of speech or of wisdom, declaring unto you the testimony of God.

2 For I determined not to know any thing among you, save Jesus Christ, and him crucified.

3 And I was with you in weakness, and in fear, and in much trembling.

4 And my speech and my preaching was not with enticing words of man's wisdom, but in demonstration of the Spirit and of power:

5 THAT YOUR FAITH SHOULD NOT STAND IN THE WISDOM OF MEN, BUT IN THE POWER OF GOD.

You should put your faith in God instead of in men or women, because God's power will never fail. Humans will fail you, but *God* will never fail you. Circumstances have to change when you put your faith in the power of God, because His power cannot fail.

Electricity is a powerful substance. But even so, from time to time the electricity in your house goes out. Something may have happened to the power plant that supplies your house with electricity; someone may have hit a transformer; or a storm may have knocked down power lines. At any given time, the lights in your house may go off, because that power can fail you. But the power of God will *never* fail you.

It's time for Christians to start putting our faith in the power of God instead of in the wisdom of men! Sometimes when you're believing God for something, you might even put your faith in what you're believing God for. For example, if you're believing God for a financial blessing, you might tend to put your faith in your savings account. Or you might start looking to your job to be your source. But no matter what you're believing God for, always put your faith in *God* and *His* power.

It was the power of God that created the universe, so we know that the power of God works! When you have your faith in that kind of power, how can you doubt? There is no room for doubt when your faith is in the power of God, because you've seen what the power of God can do. His power cannot and will not fail. Hallelujah!

Man's wisdom is very limited, but God's wisdom is unlimited. And the Holy Ghost can do more for you in just two seconds than man's wisdom can do for you in an eternity. That is why the Bible says that your faith should not stand in the wisdom of man but in the power of God. God's power is mighty, and faith is the key to having His power operate in your life.

I grew up in a home where faith was taught. My grandfather, Rev. Kenneth E. Hagin, preached faith. My dad, Rev. Kenneth Hagin Jr., preached faith. And I've probably heard more faith sermons than anyone on earth! From the time I was an infant crawling on my knees, I've been in church hearing faith taught night after night after night and day after day after day.

But it's not enough to hear about faith as a child growing up. You have to hear about faith and keep hearing about it. In just the last few years, the Lord has revealed so much more to me about faith than I ever knew before. And this revelation has literally changed my family's life and ministry.

I'd heard First Corinthians 2:1-5 over and over again, because it is one of the theme scripture references for Rev. Kenneth E. Hagin's Holy Ghost Meetings. When I travel with him to the Holy Ghost Meetings, I sit in two services a day for two or three weeks. Yet it took about six or seven Holy Ghost Meetings for the light to go on, so to speak, and for me to hear this passage in a brand-new way.

I realized that it's not enough to just *have* faith. You have to have faith *in* something. First Corinthians 2:5

says, *"That your faith should not stand in the wisdom of men, but in the power of God."* That means if you're believing God in a certain situation, then you need to believe that the power of God is going to turn that situation around!

'Let There Be'

The Book of Genesis tells us that in the beginning the earth was without form and void. Then God said, "Let there be light!" And there was light. God said, "Let there be animals, mountains, trees . . ." and so forth. Every time the Lord said, "Let there be" — there *was*! He spoke the Word, and His power made it happen.

When you see anything in this earth — mountains, trees, oceans, and valleys — you are seeing what the power of God can do. If you put your faith in His power, you're going to get your answer! I didn't say, "You *might* get it." I didn't say, "*Maybe* you will get it" or "*If* it's the Lord's will, you'll get it," because it *is* the

Lord's will. And if you put your faith in God's power, you *will* get your answer, because God cannot and will not fail.

God's Word Works

One day at a Holy Ghost Meeting, I realized that according to First Corinthians 2:5, my faith must be in the power of God. At that time, everything in my life was going pretty well. But I wanted to test the Scripture. In other words, I wanted to prove it out and watch God perform His Word on my behalf.

So while I was meditating on putting my faith in the power of God, I said to Him, "Lord, there is something that I want." Remember, the Lord said He would give us the desires of our heart (Ps. 37:4). I told Him I wanted a new set of golf clubs.

I didn't really need them, but they were what I desired at the time. And to be honest with you, I was financially able at that time to just go out and buy the clubs, but because they weren't a necessity, I decided to test this scripture and believe God for them.

> **MATTHEW 18:19**
> **19 Again I say unto you, That if two of you shall agree on earth as touching any thing that they shall ask, it shall be done for them of my Father which is in heaven.**

Here we read that the Bible says, "If two of you shall agree as touching *anything* . . . ." So, obviously, if you want another person to agree with you, you have to find someone like-minded with like faith. If you want someone to agree with you for something, and the person doesn't really care whether or not you get what you're believing for, then he or she is not like-minded and of like faith.

It's good to have someone to pray the prayer of agreement with you, and it's also biblical. But it's *even better* to find someone who will not only pray the prayer of agreement with you, but who will also hang in there with you until your answer manifests.

So I asked my best friend who also desired a new set of golf clubs to agree with me. I *knew* he was of like-mind and like-faith, so he and I got together and agreed in prayer. Remember, Matthew 18:19 says that when two people come together to agree they should *ask*. You see, many people are doing the *agreeing* part, but they forget the *asking* part. The Bible says, "You have not because you ask not" (James 4:2). Sometimes our mind says, "Well, Lord, You know what my desires are because You know everything." Yes, He does know everything, but He's waiting for you to ask Him for what you want.

So I asked God for a set of golf clubs, and then I prayed the prayer of agreement with my friend of like-faith. If you are a golfer, then you know that steel shafts are less expensive than graphite shafts. I only had "steel-shaft faith" at that time, so I needed enough money to be able to buy a new set of steel-shaft clubs. I put my faith in the power of God and began believing for enough money to come in.

The week after I prayed, I went to Colorado for a convention where different companies come together to sell their merchandise at whole-sale prices to various churches and bookstores.

I went to a record-company booth located near our Faith Library Publications booth, and they were having a *putting* contest as an advertising gimmick. The putt to make was thirty feet long, and the prize was $500 cash! The man who organized the contest had considered the law of averages, and going by man's wis-dom, he determined that only one, maybe two, might actually make the putt during the course of the week.

So I walked up and used their putter, which wasn't very good. The "hole" was set up on artificial turf that sort of moved around as I stepped on it. But I walked up to make my "putt of faith"! I took the putter back, hit the ball, and it went straight into the hole!

I was the first person to even walk up to the booth to enter the contest. The man working there couldn't believe it. His mouth flew wide open! I immediately told him my testimony. I told him that the $500 was going to go toward my new set of golf clubs!

Now let me tell you the rest of the putting contest story! A friend of mine who was with me at the booth stepped up right after me and sunk *his* putt for $500. He was on his way to the mission field at the time and needed $500 to move to Mexico. He was as excited as I was!

Needless to say, the man working the record-company's booth immediately changed the contest. From then on, instead of giving the winners $500 cash, they were going to award $500 worth of merchandise. But *no one else* during the entire rest of the week made the putt. Out of nearly 30,000 people at the convention, not one more person made that putt. You see, when I putted, it wasn't just a normal putt — I was in *faith*! I was in faith, not only for the putt to go in, but for my new golf clubs!

It might sound as if God used a weird thing to bring me money, but it doesn't matter what He uses. I'm not concerned about how God answers my prayers. Too many people get concerned about *how* God is going to meet their needs. They might say, "Well, Uncle So-and-so has a lot of money. Maybe God will speak to *him*."

I am not concerned about where the money's coming from. I just put my faith in the power of God. I know He is my Source, and I don't tell Him how to do things. I let Him do things the way He wants to do them.

Manifested Blessings

My birthday was the week after the convention, and people who usually forgot my birthday gave me *money*! Money poured in all over the place, because that's the way God is.

He does things abundantly above all we can ask or think (Eph. 3:20)! He never does "just enough." Our God is a God who is *more than enough*! Too many Christians are believing God for just enough. We need to start believing for more than enough. In the span of just a few weeks, I went from believing God for my golf clubs to having them. And God is *not* a respecter of persons. If He will do it for me, He will do it for you too.

Some people miss out on their blessing because they think faith manifests the blessing overnight. So after they pray and don't see results, they give up. But when I started believing God for my golf clubs, I didn't just say one prayer of agreement. Instead, each time I thought about the new clubs I wanted, I would say, "Thank You, Lord, for my new golf clubs." And when I played with my old golf clubs, after each shot I hit, I would say, "Thank You, Lord, for my new golf clubs." And I kept thanking Him, because as far as I was concerned, I already had them by faith. There was no doubt in my mind that they were coming, because I put my faith in the power of God.

When it was all said and done, I had more than enough money to buy the more expensive graphite shafts instead of steel shafts. And I also bought a five-wood, which I had been needing. Then I bought some shoes and other odds and ends and just had a good ol' golfing time! All of this happened because I received revelation on First Corinthians 2:5, which says, *"That your faith should not stand in the wisdom of men, but in the power of God."*

Opportunities for Blessing

Remember, God does not have favorites. He wants you to put your faith in His power, too, because if you do, He will be able to do great things for you. Your faith may start with something small, such as golf clubs, but when you see the power of God demonstrated in your life, you will be able to believe God for even bigger and better things.

After I had proved the Word of God by believing for and receiving a new set of golf clubs, I knew that First Corinthians 2:5 would work in any area of life. And I began to put my faith in the power of God for other things — including *a brand-new house*! Remember, God's power created the universe. Nothing is impossible with Him (Luke 1:37)!

When I was believing God for my house, I had attacks coming against me! Some people said, "You can't build a house that big. People will start saying that you're too young to have a house that big." And I was faced with a choice. I could put my faith in their wisdom, which was the wisdom of man. And I could start saying, "Yes, maybe they're right. Maybe I shouldn't build a house that big. Maybe I am too young."

When those attacks started coming against me, I had an opportunity to lose the house that I was believing for! Now in the natural, I didn't *have* the house to lose it — I was believing for the house by faith! But I had an opportunity to lose it, because I could have started listening to the wisdom of men. I couldn't put my faith in the wisdom of man and in the power of God at the same time. I had to choose. But I knew that only one would bring me my house — faith in the *power of God*.

You will have the same opportunity when you're believing God for things, whether they be spiritual, physical, or financial blessings. If you have sickness in your body and you're hurting, someone might say to you, "Well, I don't know if it's God's will for you to be healed." Or, "Maybe God put that sickness on you to teach you a lesson." But that's just the wisdom of men.

You have to stand up and say, "I don't care what man says. I don't care what it looks like. I don't care what it *feels* like. All I care about is putting my faith in the power of God and coming out of this situation victorious!" You have to be that bold about it. The Bible says, "If you can believe it, you shall receive it" (Matt. 21:22)! But you have to believe it.

If you want the power of God to work for you, you have to have faith, because without it you can't please God (Heb. 11:6). And you have to be a giver. Some people don't like to hear about giving, but the Bible says that the first ten-percent of your income belongs to God (Lev. 27:30). If you're not paying your tithes, then you might be blessed *in a measure*, but the windows of heaven will not be opened up for you. The Bible says, "When you bring your tithes to the storehouse, the windows of heaven will be opened, and God will pour out a blessing that you *cannot contain*" (Mal. 3:10). It's time for you to enter into the blessings of God. Being blessed is a decision that you have to make. And it begins by your decision to use your faith.

Now I see faith in a brand-new light. Seeing faith this way has utterly changed my life. And it has changed what I am able to believe God for. I went from believing for day-to-day things, to believing for a new set of golf clubs, to being able to believe Him for a brand-new dream house. The Lord had been saying, "Craig, trust Me. Trust Me! Just see what I can do!" Now I have seen and experienced God's power not only in the spiritual realm, but in the natural realm as well. And the blessings of God have just been incredible.

My blessings began before I ever had a new set of golf clubs or a brand-new house. My blessings began when I began believing in faith. Faith in what? Faith in golf clubs? Faith in houses? No! I put my faith in the *power of God*!

Faith Is the Key

Faith is the key to having the power of God work in your life. But it's just as important to know *where to put your faith*. The Word of God says in First Corinthians 2:5 that your faith should be in the *power of*

God, not the wisdom of men. If you want to have the power of God move on your behalf, you have to have faith. You have to have faith not only in the power, but you also have to have faith to "step out" when the power is present.

Remember, we are supposed to put our faith in the power of God, not in things or in people. As I've said, many times when Christians are believing God for something, such as healing, they begin to put their faith in the healing or whatever they're believing for. Don't put your faith in the thing itself — put your faith in God and His power.

And don't limit God by telling Him how you want the answer to manifest. People are always trying to tell God what channels to use. Instead, have the attitude, *God, it doesn't matter how You want to do it. Any way is fine with me, because I'm just here to receive.* Don't be concerned with the how's, because that part is up to God. Let *Him* take care of the how's. You just take care of the receiving and rejoicing parts!

Those are the fun parts, and they go together. You rejoice before, during, and after you receive. You rejoice *before,* because whenever you ask God for anything in faith, you actually receive it at the time that you pray.

There have been many things that I've believed God for that I rejoiced over daily before they ever manifested in this natural realm. I mentioned how I would rejoice each time I hit a ball with my old golf clubs. I also rejoiced *before* my new house was ever built. I owned the piece of property, but there wasn't a house on the land. My wife and I believed God that we would one day live in a house on that piece of land. I would regularly pull up on the street where my house was going to be. I would look over that lot, and I could "see" my house there — even when it wasn't there! No, it wasn't there physically, but it was there by faith. I knew my house was going to be built right there. I knew it just like I knew my name. When you are standing in faith, you have to be that confident. And you *can* be when your faith is in the power of God.

Then there came the day when the house was there physically. I walked in the front door, still rejoicing! I had a brand-new house. And because God does things abundantly above all we can ask or think, I walked into a brand-new house with brand-new furniture, brand-new drapes — brand-new everything! That's what having faith in the power of God can do!

Chapter 2
Actions of Faith

Remember, no matter what your circumstances look like, how you're feeling, or how much money you owe — whatever you're going through — God has your answer!

If you are a Christian, then victory belongs to you. Healing belongs to you. Prosperity belongs to you. All these things are yours because they belong to God. And anything that belongs to Him belongs to you. He's given it to you!

Any adverse situation or problem you might be facing must fall because God has already provided the answer for it. There is nothing that any person or any demon — on the earth or under the earth — can do about it. Victory is yours! It's time to start thanking God for what belongs to you!

The trials you face don't determine your outcome. There might be certain situations in my own life that from the natural standpoint don't look good. But I'm not looking with natural eyes! I can look from the *supernatural* standpoint. With supernatural eyes, I can see the end result — *I win*! I win, not because I'm anything spectacular, but because I serve a spectacular God! My God has already provided for me! And before I can see the victory with my *physical* eyes, I can see it with my *spiritual* eyes.

If you will close your eyes and begin looking at your circumstances and problems through the eyes of faith, you will see those things deteriorating. Then it won't be long before you can open your *physical* eyes and see those problems deteriorating in the natural realm as well. Some Christians wait until the answer manifests in the natural realm before they start getting excited. It's okay to be excited then, *too*, but you need to be excited *before* then!

You should start getting excited about it when you pray, because if you pray *expecting*, then you know beyond a shadow of doubt that the problems have to leave. They have no right to bother or hinder you because you are God's property. Satan has no authority over God's property. Satan *cannot* and *will not* touch God's property when you are in faith.

If you are God's property, and Satan cannot legally touch God's property, then Satan cannot touch *you* — unless you let him. Too many people open the door and give Satan a way into their lives. But if you don't let him in, he has no right to so much as put his foot in the door of your life!

Circumstances Are Temporary

During this life on earth, you are going to have trials. But here's the good news: You can always come out on top! A man once asked my grandfather, Rev. Kenneth E. Hagin, to agree with him in prayer that he wouldn't have any more trials, because he was tired of facing them. My grandfather asked him if he was ready to die, and the man said no. So my grandfather told him, "Well, the only way you're not going to face any more trials is to go to heaven today, because the only place there aren't any trials is up in heaven."

There are trials in this world because Satan is the god of this world. But it doesn't matter who the god of this world is, because with God on your side, you're going over the top! In *every* situation and circumstance, you can go over the top if you go with God.

Things in the natural are only temporal. Circumstances will not last forever because they are only temporary. Don't let trials get the best of you. From now on, every time you face an adverse situation or circumstance, think of it as another opportunity to put your faith into action.

Think of it as just another chance to believe God and build

your faith. You see, the devil is trying to destroy you, but really he's *helping* you because he's giving you an opportunity to build your faith. Then the next time he comes around, your fight of faith will be easier, because you have been building your faith up.

Begin to look at problems as another way to build yourself up in God. Look at the bright side and turn bad things to good things. Focusing on the positives will keep you away from the negatives.

God Is *More* Than Enough!

It helps to remember that circumstances are only temporal. But the *greatest* thing to remember when you're faced with a problem is that you serve a God who is *more than enough*! He is able to bless you abundantly above all you can ask or think!

We as Christians serve a "more than" God. Whatever we need, He gives us *more than*! We're not serving a "barely enough" or "almost enough" God. We're serving a *"more than enough"* God!

Put your faith in the power of God. The power of God *cannot* and *will not* fail. There is no power greater than the power of God. His is the most awesome power in the universe. And when you're believing God concerning your situations and circumstances, that means you're putting your faith in His awesome power!

Whatever you need, God has your answer. You don't have to wait until tomorrow or the next day to get it. God has it now! And if God has it, *you* can have it. It *belongs* to you, because whatever belongs to God belongs to you.

Reach Out and Receive

My dad, Rev. Kenneth Hagin Jr., has acquired many different possessions over the years. Some of them are a lot of fun, especially the water craft — or "water toys," as I like to call them. My favorite is his ski boat, which I consider to be my own!

My dad bought it, so technically it's his boat. But if anyone asks whose boat it is, I tell them it's mine. His name is on the title, but it's my boat!

You see, anything that belongs to my father, as far as I'm concerned, belongs to me too. I can use anything that belongs to him because he has told me repeatedly, "Son, what's mine is yours." One day when he was out of town preaching, we got a few inches of snow in Broken Arrow, Oklahoma, where I live. Because my dad was preaching out of the state, I figured he didn't need his brand-new 4 x 4 vehicle. So I went over to his house and borrowed it!

When he came home, I told him I had borrowed his truck. He said, "I meant to call you and tell you that if it snowed to go over and get it." You see, as far as he's concerned, whatever is his belongs to me. He's overjoyed to know that I feel free to use his possessions. He's proud that he's able to share them with me.

I am the same with my sons. Whatever my wife and I have belongs to them — our whole household. And it's the same way with God. Whatever belongs to God belongs to us. As His children, we have the legal right to appropriate what belongs to God.

That means we don't have to ask Him for permission every time we want to be healed. We don't have to say, "Lord, can I borrow some healing?" or "Lord, can I borrow some financial blessings?" All we have to do is take hold of it, because God's Word has already promised it to us. It already belongs to us through Jesus Christ!

Because Jesus died, our sins were forgiven. Because He died, we are able to have heaven as our eternal home. And because stripes were laid upon His back as He died upon the Cross, we were healed and made whole two thousand years ago. It all belongs to us: salvation, healing, and prosperity. It's already been bought and paid for. We don't

have to pay for it, and we don't have
to beg and plead for it. All we have
to do is remind God of what He's
done for us, and take hold of what
belongs to us.

Sometimes I have to remind my
dad when he's forgotten things he's
promised me. But God doesn't forget the things He promised you. He
always remembers them. Sometimes we have to remind our earthly
fathers and say, "Dad, you promised
this. It belongs to me, and I'm taking hold of it."

That's the same thing we have to
do in our spirit. We find a scripture
to stand on, and we say, "Lord, in
your Word You said all of my needs
are met. You said that nothing is
impossible with You" (Phil. 4:19;
Luke 1:37).

Remember, whatever God has
belongs to you, and all you have to
do is just "reach out" and take what
you need. It's your legal right to
take what belongs to you! So if you
need a miracle, reach out and take
hold of it. If you need healing, reach

out and take hold of that healing. If
you need a financial blessing, then
reach out and take hold of it!

Keep Pushing On and
Pressing In

In Luke chapter 5 and Mark
chapter 2, we have two accounts of
the man who was sick with the
palsy. The sick man's friends
brought him to Jesus to be healed.
But when they arrived at the house
where Jesus was preaching, they
could not get into the room because
of the crowd.

LUKE 5:17-20
**17 And it came to pass on a
certain day, as he was teach-
ing, that there were Pharisees and doctors of the law
sitting by, which were come
out of every town of Galilee,
and Judaea, and Jerusalem:
and the power of the Lord
was present to heal them.
18 And, behold, men brought
in a bed a man which was
taken with a palsy: and they
sought means to bring him**

in, and to lay him before him
[Jesus].
19 And when they could not
find by what way they
might bring him in because
of the multitude, they went
upon the housetop, and let
him down through the
tiling with his couch into
the midst before Jesus.
20 And when he saw their
faith, he said unto him, Man,
thy sins are forgiven thee.

These men were only concerned about one thing: getting their friend healed. The four men didn't care what happened — they were going to do *whatever* they had to do for their friend to receive his healing. The perfect plan was for them to carry him into the room and set him right down before Jesus. Instead, they were forced to go to "Plan B." But they weren't worried about it; they just kept on going.

When Christians are believing God in a particular situation and something happens contrary to what they were expecting or believing, they sometimes think, *Oh no, I've missed it somewhere.* They just fall apart and never receive whatever it was they were believing for. But, you see, even when you are facing contrary circumstances, you still have to keep pressing on and pushing in. You have to keep doing whatever it takes to receive what you need from God.

Mark 2:4 says, *"And when they could not come nigh unto him for the press, they uncovered the roof where he was: and when they had broken it up, they let down the bed wherein the sick of the palsy lay."*

When it looked as if there was no way for the man with the palsy to get into the room where Jesus was, he kept pushing on and pressing in. His friends tore the roof off in order to get him to Jesus. You have to be the same way. When everything has gone wrong, and everything looks bad instead of good, you can't give up. Of course, "Plan A" was for everything to go perfectly. But sometimes some trials and struggles come. But you keep pressing on and believing in spite of what's going on around you.

The Power of God Was Present To Heal *Everyone*

Now in Luke 5:17 says, *". . . the power of the Lord was present to heal them."* "Them" means everyone who was present in the room! So we know that the power of God was present to heal everyone in the room. But we have no record of any man coming to Jesus except for this one with the palsy who was let down through the roof.

Why was he the only one who came to Jesus and the only one healed if the power of God was present to heal them all? *He was the only one healed because he was the only one who had faith in the power of God!* As soon as Jesus saw his faith, He said to him, "Your sins are forgiven."

You see, it took faith to go to the roof, and it took faith to tear the roof off. It took faith to be lowered down in the crowd. The sick man

and his four friends had put their
faith in the power of God. They were
willing to do whatever it took to
reach Jesus and receive healing.

Don't Listen to Doubt

The Pharisees and teachers of
the Law were telling Jesus, "No,
Jesus, you're doctrinally off. You
can't heal on the Sabbath Day." But
Jesus didn't listen to them. There
might be people who try to speak
doubt into your life too. They will
say, "You can't do this, and you can't
do that." But you don't have to listen to them. You can choose to listen
to doubt if you want to, but if you
do, you will miss out.

Jesus chose not to listen, and the
man with the palsy chose not to listen. You see, it probably wasn't
"proper" for the four friends to tear
the roof off or to let the man down
right in the middle of Jesus' preaching! But they did it anyway, and,
immediately, Jesus saw the man's
faith and said, "Son, thy sins are
forgiven." Then the Pharisees and

teachers of the Law said, "Jesus, you can't forgive a man's sin."

Jesus rebuked all of them and then told the man, "Rise up and walk" (Luke 5:23). Now think about it: This man came into the room on a bed lowered from the roof, but he left the room by walking out the door — totally healed! This healing was a great miracle, but he was the only one who was healed. The power of the Lord was present to heal them *all*, but everyone else was worried about what the Pharisees and the teachers of the Law would think and say about them. So they missed out.

Don't listen to the doubt and unbelief that people try to discourage you with. Just keep pressing in to Jesus. And no matter how bad the circumstances around you are, keep putting your faith in the power of God.

Faith *Expects*!

If you are believing God for something, get excited about it *now*!

Don't leave all the dancing and shouting for later. Start dancing and shouting *now*. Because we *know* that our God does not lie (Heb. 6:18)! We are not *hoping* so. We are not saying, "Well, maybe if we pray enough and do all the right things." No, we *know*. We know that our God has promised us victory, healing, and prosperity! And since these things belong to us, we should pray *expecting* to receive them.

While we're expecting to receive, we can shout and dance and have a Holy Ghost time, because we have already seen our outcome with the eye of faith! We might not see the manifestation tomorrow or the next day, but we can know it's on the way.

Just as the man in the Gospels who was sick with the palsy, we can *expect* an answer from God. His friends let him down through a hole in the roof of the house where Jesus was ministering, because they were expecting him to be healed.

It took a lot of faith for the sick man's friends to take him to the top of the house, tear the roof off, and lower him down in the middle of a church service. When the man came down, Jesus saw his faith and said, *". . . Arise, and take up thy couch, and go into thine house"* (Luke 5:24). Likewise, *your* faith can make *you* whole. The power of God is present to heal you! Healing belongs to you, because God has already provided it for you. But whether or not you get healed is up to you and your faith.

'Turn On the Faucet'

It's time for us to take hold of the healing that has been provided for us through Jesus Christ. Remember, it's the power of God that heals you.

I like to use a practical illustration to help explain how the healing power of God works. In this illustration, I associate running water, such as the kind that flows out of a household faucet, with the healing power of God, and I associate the faucet with Christians.

If you have running water in your house, then your sink or bathtub has what is called a faucet. It's the pipe that the water comes out of. People are kind of like the faucet — just a vessel the water flows through. The water is not actually *stored* in your faucet; it's in a tank or lake or well that's located somewhere else. And it is pumped to you *through* the faucet.

Just like water in a faucet, the healing power of God is not *stored* in an individual; it's stored in God. But it is pumped *through* an individual.

To illustrate this a little further, the water only runs through the faucet when we turn the knob to the "on" position. If we leave the knob in the "off" position, we'll never have any water. We could pray and believe God for water, but until we turn the knob, we will never have any water. In the same way, we as Christians must "turn on the faucet" in order for the healing power of God to flow through us. How do we turn on the faucet spiritually speaking? *By faith.* We just say, "Lord, I thank You for my healing. I put my trust in You."

Chapter 3
The 'Greater' Mentality

It's not enough to know that God is powerful. We need to *put our faith* in that awesome power and begin to act upon our faith. And we also need to have what I call a "greater mentality." We obtain a "greater" mentality by understanding and dwelling on the greatness of God until His greatness becomes a reality in our life and we see the power of God as *greater* than our problem or circumstance. Unfortunately, many times when we're facing challenges, our thinking gets a little backward and we start talking about how great our *problems* are and how great the *obstacles* are. We need to remember that they are nothing compared to the greatness of God! And, according to the Bible, we have the *Greater One* living on the inside of us!

1 JOHN 4:4
4 Ye are of God, little children, and have overcome them: because GREATER is he that is in you, than he that is in the world.

Problems and negative circumstances are like speed bumps. A speed bump is made to slow you down when you are going too fast. And, really, a speed bump might slow you down a little bit, but it never causes you to come to a complete stop. You always keep on going. It's the same way with the problems we face. The devil has designed them to slow us down when we get going too fast for the Kingdom of God and he feels threatened. But we can ride right over them and keep on going because the Greater One lives in us!

We need to have the "greater" mentality. We serve a big God, and He is greater than the devil. When it comes down to it, the devil is tiny. He tries to act big, but he's not!

There were a number of people whom I knew growing up who were not that big physically, but they always tried to act real big. One guy in my high school physical education class was nicknamed "Peanut." Of course, he wasn't very big — that's why he got the nickname "Peanut" — but he had a big mouth on him! And that's the way the devil is. He tries to get in your face and hinder you, but he has no real authority. Jesus took all authority away from him two thousand years ago.

But so many Christians are letting the devil defeat them. They are distraught, depressed and worried about so many things. But we need to have the *greater* mentality. Instead of worrying about problems, difficulties, and what the devil might try to do, we need to start thinking about God and what *He* can do. We concentrate on God and His power by praising Him.

So start thinking about the Greater One instead of the "little

one" — the devil. When you spend
your time thinking about the
Greater One, you will begin to get
the greater mentality. And then you
will realize that with the Greater
One on the inside of you, you cannot
fail!

David and Goliath

There is a story in First Samuel
chapter 17 that really illustrates
what I'm talking about. It's the
account of David and Goliath. You
may have heard it before, but it
would do you good to remember it
more often — especially when
you're facing your own Goliath.

David was just a seventeen year-
old boy, and Goliath was a giant
who had successfully taunted the
entire army of Israel. Goliath had
challenged them to find anyone who
could defeat him in combat. Everyone in Israel was worried and
afraid. They were panicking
because they didn't know what to
do. All they could see was a giant
whom no one could beat. But they

were only looking at the outward appearance.

Faith doesn't look on the outside. When you are in faith, you aren't moved by what you see. You aren't moved by the outward appearance of circumstances. You see, with God, it doesn't matter what it looks like on the outside. All that matters is what's on the inside. And since you have the Greater One on the inside (1 John 4:4), you are greater than whatever comes your way. You can't ever face anything that is greater than God.

Even though David was a young boy, he knew how powerful his God was. And even though he was only a shepherd, he volunteered to fight Goliath. Everyone told him that he would be defeated, but he wouldn't be talked out of fighting.

Go With What You Know

King Saul finally said, "Well, if you're going out there, let me put my armor on you. You can't go out there and fight without any weapons." But

Saul was bigger physically than David, and his armor didn't fit. David wasn't used to armor of any kind, because he had never worn armor before. He had only been in battles with a lion and a bear that had tried to mess with his sheep. He defeated them both with just a sling and a rod.

So David said he would rather fight Goliath with his own weapons. He told Saul, "I have to go with what I know. And all I know is my sling and my rod. So I'm going to fight with what I've got."

We can learn something from David's decision. You see, many times when Christians get into difficulties and things look bad, they start looking around for someone else's "armor" to fight the devil with. In other words, they try to find out what other Christians did when they were in a similar situation. But it doesn't matter what anyone else did. You have to do what *you* know to do and handle it the way *you* know how to handle it. You can't depend on the way someone else fought the battle, because if you lose the battle, you will blame it on someone else. But it's not anyone's battle but your own. And, even then, your battle is not really yours, but the Lord's (2 Chron. 20:15).

1 SAMUEL 17:40-44

40 And he [David] took his staff in his hand, and chose him five smooth stones out of the brook, and put them in a shepherd's bag which he had, even in a scrip; and his sling was in his hand: and he drew near to the Philistine.

41 And the Philistine came on and drew near unto David; and the man that bare the shield went before him.

42 And when the Philistine looked about, and saw David, he disdained him: for he was but a youth, and ruddy, and of a fair countenance.

43 And the Philistine said unto David, Am I a dog, that

**thou comest to me with
staves? And the Philistine
cursed David by his gods.
44 And the Philistine said
to David, Come to me, and I
will give thy flesh unto the
fowls of the air, and to the
beasts of the field.**

Goliath was asking, "Am I a dog
that you would come at me with a
bunch of sticks? Your sticks aren't
going to harm me at all. And that
sling ain't going to do you any good.
I've defied all of the armies of Israel,
and they won't come fight me, yet
you come out with a sling and a
stick!" Goliath was talking big! And
sometimes the devil starts talking
real big to us too. Circumstances
don't look good, and the devil starts
saying, "What are you going to do?
It's all over. You can't make that pay-
ment. You're not even going to make
enough on your job this week to feed
your family." Or he will say, "That
cancer in your body is going to kill
you, and there's nothing you can do
about it. There's not a doctor that
can help you. You've gone down too

far." The devil does the same thing today to Christians that Goliath did to David in the Old Testament. And we must do the same thing to the devil that David did to Goliath!

1 SAMUEL 17:45-47
45 Then said David to the Philistine, Thou comest to me with a sword, and with a spear, and with a shield: BUT I COME TO THEE IN THE NAME OF THE LORD OF HOSTS, THE GOD OF THE ARMIES OF ISRAEL, whom thou hast defied.
46 This day will the Lord deliver thee into mine hand; and I will smite thee, and take thine head from thee; and I will give the carcases of the host of the Philistines this day unto the fowls of the air, and to the wild beasts of the earth; that all the earth may know that there is a God in Israel.
47 And all this assembly shall know that the Lord saveth not with sword and spear: FOR THE BATTLE IS

THE LORD'S, and he will give you into our hands.

David didn't just come with a sling and a staff, he came with the full backing of the Greater One — the One who created the heavens and the earth. Goliath had big muscles, and a big sword too. But those were just natural weapons. David came with the *power of God*! And God's power is greater than any natural weapon.

Don't Taunt God

Goliath had been defying the Lord. He had been saying, "The Lord isn't going to deliver you. You're going down."

In athletic competition, such as in a football or basketball game, the players on opposing teams might taunt each other, and they might receive a slight penalty for doing it. But don't taunt God — the penalty will be *much more* severe.

It's never wise to taunt or mess with God. When the devil messes with us, he's messing with God, because we're children of God! In a natural family, whenever a person messes with someone's family, the head of the family steps up and says, "Don't mess with my children." It's the same way when the devil messes with one of God's children.

David approached Goliath with the full power of God. Goliath had some talk, but that's all it was — *talk*. However, David backed up his talk with *action*. He said, "I'm coming with the power of the Almighty God, and you're going down!" Then he pulled out his sling, let one stone fly, and he killed Goliath.

Notice that David did what he knew how to do. He did everything he could in the natural to win the battle. He didn't sit in a corner ducking his head, saying, "God, save me from this Philistine!" He put his faith in the power of God and acted upon that faith!

Unfortunately, many Christians today aren't doing what they already know to do in the natural to conquer their problems. They are waiting for God to do everything. And, instead of holding out the shield of faith and marching on, they are ducking in the corner, hiding. But you don't have to hide any longer. You can boldly stand against the devil because Jesus gave you the right and authority to do so.

David boldly put one stone in his sling and gave it a fling using all of his natural strength. And as that stone came out of his sling, it gained momentum. That stone left his hand with only natural power, but it gained *supernatural* power as it landed in the skull of the Philistine. David knocked Goliath dead with just one stone!

So when you're facing a challenge, do everything you know how to do in the natural. Then let God take care of the rest. In the natural, a sling wasn't enough power to kill that Philistine. It would have made him mad, and it might have stung a little bit. But as my dad says, "When you mix the natural and the supernatural together, it makes an explosive force for God!" When you have the "greater" mentality, you won't back away from a challenge. With your faith in the power of God and the Greater One within you, you will rise to the occasion, face the challenge, and win!

Shadrach, Meshach, And Abednego

In Daniel chapter 3, the Hebrew boys Shadrach, Meshach, and Abednego had a few challenges. Their first challenge was to stay true to God even when King Nebuchadnezzar demanded that everyone bow to the idol he had made.

King Nebuchadnezzar ordered that everyone bow to the idol whenever the music played. But Shadrach, Meshach, and Abednego chose not to bow. Now there were other people in that crowd who believed just as they did. But when the music played, only three guys remained standing. Why? They decided to take a stand for what they believed. The rest of them didn't stand for what they believed, and they avoided persecution by the king. But they had to repent later.

Unfortunately, many Christians today have the "repent later" mentality. They think they can lie to some guy, sell him an old junk automobile, for example, and just repent for it later. Or someone might say, "I could do something so that So-and-so doesn't get the promotion he's up for. And I can just repent about it later." Many times, instead of facing the challenge and accepting the difficulties that go along with it by doing what they know is right to do, many Christians bow down under the pressure.

Of course, you can truly repent, and the Lord will forgive you, but how much greater it is to stand up for what is right according to the Word of God. When you make a stand for God, you will receive a greater blessing in the end.

Shadrach, Meshach, and Abednego stood up for what they believed even though it meant they would be thrown in the fiery furnace to die. They told the king, "You might kill us, but we will never bow. Our God said we must never bow to any other god, and we choose to obey His commands. So do what you may; we're not bowing."

They didn't care what the king or anyone else thought. They only cared about pleasing God. Some people today have a "What's everyone else doing?" mentality. Instead of having the *greater* mentality, they always have to know what someone else is doing. That is succumbing to peer pressure, and being a man-pleaser. As Christians, we ought to be *God*-pleasers (Gal. 1:10).

Don't Bow Under Pressure

It doesn't matter what anyone else is doing. Each person will have to deal with his or her own conscience and answer to God for what he or she did. You only have to deal with *your* conscience and answer to God for *your* actions.

Shadrach, Meshach, and Abed-nego stood even though everyone else was bowing. So the king was furious, and he heated the furnace seven times hotter than ever before. The Bible tells us that the men who threw the three Hebrew boys into the flames died just from the heat (Dan. 3:22). King Nebuchadnezzar and his men stood nearby to watch them burn. When the king looked, instead of seeing three men, he saw *four*! And the fourth looked like the Son of God!

Then King Nebuchadnezzar had the boys taken out of the fire, and he changed his tune. He decided that the Hebrew boys' God was the real God, and he made a decree that everyone had to serve the God of Shadrach, Meshach, and Abed-nego. Because they didn't bow under pressure, *greater* things happened to them, and they were allowed to worship the one true God (*See* Daniel chapter 6).

The Fourth Man in the Fire

When you are in the midst of the fire of persecution or problems, the

Lord is there with you. When it looks as if there is no way out, He will make a way of deliverance. He says, "I will never leave you nor forsake you" (Heb. 13:5). Whatever difficulties you may be facing, He is right there with you to help you along the way.

He is there to make a way of escape. But you have to stand tall and trust Him even when it looks as if there's no way! Even when it looks like you are going under! Put your faith in the power of God and trust Him anyway!

It looked as if Shadrach, Meshach, and Abednego were going under. In the natural, there was no way out. They were going to burn to death, but God delivered them. They came out of the fire and didn't even smell like smoke! Their clothes and their hair weren't singed. That's a great miracle in itself. But an even greater miracle is that they walked *in* bound, but they walked *out* free!

When you're facing challenges or trials, and you feel bound up, the fiery darts of the enemy may be

your fiery furnace. Just remember
that the Lord your God is there with
you every step of the way. And He
has made a way of escape for you.
Continue to trust Him, believing
that "greater is He that is in you
than he that is in the world" (1 John
4:4)! Walk with the greater mentality, knowing that your God is
greater! And His power is greater
than any furnace you may face!

Daniel and the Lions' Den

Daniel had the same greater
mentality that Shadrach, Meshach,
and Abednego had. And in the Book
of Daniel chapter 6, he faced a similar situation. King Darius made a
law that went against what Daniel
believed. The king decreed that for
thirty days, no one was allowed to
pray to any God or man other than
to King Darius! But Daniel said,
"I'm not going to go against my God.
I'm going to stand up for what I
believe, and I'm going to pray to
Him anyway."

As punishment, the king had
Daniel thrown in the lion's den. He

stayed all night in the lions' den and was not even scratched, because God preserved him! Some people say, "He was probably running around all night trying to stay away from the lions." No, I don't think so. I think the lions were trying to stay away from *him*.

You see, *Daniel* was the greater one. He was greater than those lions. Those lions had no right or authority to harm Daniel. I think he got down there and said, "Lions, just shut your mouths. You aren't going to bother me, because I serve the Greater One. And I'm going to walk out of here as a witness to my God's power!"

Shut the Lions' Mouth!

If you're in a situation surrounded by lions, so to speak, just tell them to shut their mouths! In other words, you need to tell the devil, "No weapon formed against me shall prosper" (Isa. 54:17)! No, it's not good to get into heated conversations with the devil because there is no reason to do it. Notice that when David went to battle, he talked to Goliath, but didn't ask him any questions. He *told* Goliath what was going to happen. So don't have conversations with the devil — just tell him what's going to happen. Say, "Mr. Devil, I have the greater mentality. I'm thinking greater thoughts now — thoughts of triumph and victory. You have already been whipped, and you have no right or authority to bother me any longer. In the Name of Jesus, you have to go."

Unfortunately, instead of telling the devil where to go, many Christians "entertain" him. That doesn't mean they are having dinner with him. It just means that they allow themselves to dwell on the thoughts he puts in their mind. So, basically, they're "entertaining" him, because they are doing what he wants them to do.

Many times, the reason you are in a bad situation is that the devil has put roadblocks in your way. He's trying to detour your Christian walk. He knows the way you should be going. And he knows you *should* be having greater things down here. The devil knows that Jesus came to give you life that you might have it more abundantly (John 10:10).

But Satan will do everything he can to stop you from having an abundant, prosperous life. He's there to stop you, and if you let him, he will. You have to shut his mouth! You have to quit entertaining his thoughts. You have to quit having a poor mentality. Don't talk about how bad things are. Don't say, "I'm never going to get out of this. It's always going to be like this. I'm never going to move up any higher in life."

If you talk that way, you *won't* ever move up higher. You will never do anything that you say you will never do. So it's time to have the "greater" mentality. You are already greater on the *inside*, because the Greater One lives on the inside. But you need to get the greater mentality that's on the *inside* manifested on the *outside*!

When you have a "greater" mentality, you move up. But if you start thinking negative thoughts, it will lead to your downfall. You have to keep thinking "greater." And when it looks as if there's no way out, just holdfast to your confession of faith (Heb. 10:23). And having done all to stand, just stand (Eph. 6:13). Tell the devil, "Devil, you have no right, no authority, and no dominion over me. I'm standing on the Word of God. And the Word says I *cannot*, and I *will not* fail. I'm an overcomer through Christ Jesus. I'm the head and not the tail. I'm above and not beneath. And I'm going over."

The Devil Is a 'Has Been'

Too many folks are worrying about too many things. The reason they can't concentrate on Jesus is, they are concentrating on their problem — what the situations of life *look* or *feel* like. It's time to start concentrating on *Jesus*. Start looking to

Jesus, and when you look to Him, the situations and the problems will seem small. Remember that you serve a big God. This is the reality: big God, little devil. Our *big* God defeated the *little* devil!

The devil *has been* defeated, so that makes him just a "has been." Presently, he has no power or authority in your life other than that which you let him have. Once you realize and understand that the devil has already been whipped and that he has no power or authority against you, then you don't have to worry about what he might try to throw in your face. And when you don't have any worries or cares, you can spend your time rejoicing!

When the devil talks to you, he tries to get you all confused. He'll say, "Yeah, but doesn't it look like such-and-such is going to happen?" and "What about such-and-such? What are you going to do?" You must answer him the way Jesus did when He was tempted. He always said, "It is written . . . (Luke 4)." He never gave His own opinions. He never said, "Well Pastor So-and-so says this." He simply spoke the Word of God. That's why it's so important that we know what the Bible says.

If we don't read the Bible, we won't know what our rights are, and the devil will be able to defeat us. But if we want to have the *greater* mentality and be a greater Christian, then we have to read the Bible. Reading about people who had the greater mentality and were more than conquerors will strengthen your faith, and you, too, will be more than a conqueror through Christ Jesus (Rom. 8:37)!

Love Is Greater

If you don't walk in love, then there is no way you can have a greater mentality. Many Christians want to have Holy Ghost meetings and shout and dance, but they don't want to love one another. If you don't have love, then the running and shouting are just empty outward appearances. If you want to have a real Holy Ghost shouting time, you have to have things right on the *inside* as well.

To have the greater mentality, you have to love the brethren. You have to show compassion to other Christians. Some Christians see other believers hurting, and, instead of having compassion for them, they just walk by and say, "Well, they got what they deserve. They wouldn't even be in that mess if they hadn't done such-and-such."

Maybe they *did* do something foolish. But we can still have love and compassion toward them and help them get on the right track. Instead of judging or condemning them, we can tell them to put their faith in the power of God, because He can turn their hopeless situation around. That's walking in love. And that's what someone with the greater mentality would do.

Press Toward the Mark

As Christians, we need to love people. We need to help them let go of the past and move on to greater things. I talked to a man once who asked me to pray for him. He started by saying, "I see other Christians with joy, and I want to have some too. But I just got out of prison not too long ago. My wife left me while I was in prison." This man proceeded to tell me about all the things that had happened to him. While he was telling me about his situations and problems, I thought, *No wonder the guy doesn't have any joy. He's dwelling on the past.*

In Philippians 3:13 and 14, Paul says, *"Brethren, I count not myself to have apprehended: but this one thing I do, FORGETTING THOSE THINGS WHICH ARE BEHIND, and reaching forth unto those things which are before, I press toward the mark for the prize of the high calling of God in Christ Jesus."* You might need to forget some things from your past. If anything is weighing you down and keeping you from moving forward for God, put it behind you today. You can't change your *past*, but you can change your *future*!

Yes, this man had been to prison and his wife had left him. He had made some mistakes. But he repented, and God forgave him. So I told him to let the past go, I prayed with him, and he got the joy of the Lord on the inside of him. You see, he stopped looking at his problems and his past and started looking at the Greater One. He began to have the greater mentality.

When you're dwelling on the Greater One, you won't have a problem with your past. God is greater than your past. He is greater than your mistakes. The blood of Jesus is greater than anything you might have done. Forget the past and press toward the mark!

How to Have *Great* Days

When you have the greater mentality, even "blue days" are great days. That means that when someone asks, "How are you doing today?" you won't answer, "My sore knee's hurting a little bit, and I'm kind of tired. It's Monday, so I'm having a blue day." Instead, you will say, "Everything is *great!*"

If you have the Greater One on the inside, then you ought to be doing great! With your faith in the power of God, you can say, "It's great!" when the circumstances look bad. When it looks as if you're going under, you can say, "It's great!" When it feels as if everyone's trampling on top of you, you can say, "It's great!"

You might not like the situation you're in right now, but with the Greater One inside of you, circumstances are only temporal. Instead of looking at where you are now, keep looking at the Greater One. Start thinking greater thoughts. Start seeing greater situations. Start seeing a better way of life. For example, if your car is worn out, and you need a new one, then see yourself driving a greater car. Remember, you have to *see with the eyes of faith*. Even if in the natural it looks as if it will never come to pass, you have to see it and believe it.

When you don't have a dime to your name, see yourself with a million dollars. See yourself prosperous. If you keep seeing yourself poor, then you have a poor mentality. If you keep seeing yourself down, then you have a down mentality. To have a *greater* mentality, you have to see *greater* things in your life.

Chapter 4
You Can Have Joy in The Holy Ghost

When you are facing circumstances that test your faith, put your faith in the power of God. Remember, His power *cannot* and *will not* fail! When you have your faith in Him, you can be joyful in *any* circumstance. You will have joy when your faith is in God's power, because when you are confident of victory, *you rejoice*!

According to Scripture, we are temples of the Holy Ghost (1 Cor. 3:16; 6:19,20). And the Holy Ghost lives on the inside of us. In the Old Testament, the Holy Ghost dwelled in the temple, and if you wanted to be near the Holy Ghost, you had to go to the temple. But today, you don't have to go to church to find the Holy Ghost, because if you are a Christian, He dwells in *you*! And He is with you at all times.

If you're filled with the Holy Ghost, then you're also filled with joy. Acts 13:52 says, *"And the disciples were filled with JOY, and with the Holy Ghost."* So not only does the Holy Ghost dwell in you, but *joy* dwells in you. And if having the Holy Ghost dwelling in you makes your body the temple of the Holy Ghost, then *joy* dwelling in you means your body is a temple of *joy!* Christians are living temples of joy!

You might say, "I don't feel any joy in me." If you are a Christian, then the joy is within you whether you feel it or not. Unfortunately, many Christians go just by their feelings. But you aren't to be moved by what you feel. You are only to be moved by what you believe. The Bible says you have joy on the inside of you. That means you can rejoice even when you are in a situation that doesn't look good, simply because you have Holy Ghost joy inside you!

Count It All Joy

The Bible tells us to *count it* all joy (James 1:2). It doesn't say "It *will* be all joy when you fall into divers temptations." No, it says to *count* or *consider* it as joy. Well, how do you count it as joy? You laugh when the temptations and trials come. You can laugh because you have the Greater One on the inside, and you know that the Greater One is not going to let you down. There is no way you're going under. God is certainly not going under, and He's *with you*!

God in you cannot fail. So why should you be "down in the dumps" when you fall into divers temptation? There is no use to being down in the dumps. Someone might say, "But, brother, you don't know what it's like." Well, brother, it doesn't matter what it's like. Do you believe the Word of God or not? It's that simple. If you choose to believe God, then it doesn't *matter* what your circumstances are. Just keep believing and start counting it all joy.

I'll tell you a story about something unusual that happened one Sunday morning at my home church, RHEMA Bible Church; where I am associate pastor. Everyone was rejoicing during the service, and, suddenly, a lady in the choir started dancing, shouting, and running. She ran around the choir loft to the part of the stage where the pastoral staff sits and said to one of the pastors, "Someone stole my car this morning." Then she went on laughing and praising God. *Someone stole her car that morning*, yet she was running around the church laughing, shouting, and having a good time.

Now most people probably wouldn't have even gone to church in the first place. They would have used a stolen car as a good excuse not to go to church. And if they *did* go to church, they would have been so busy telling everyone about their car being stolen that they would have missed out on what God wanted to do in the service. But this particular lady *counted it all joy*!

Her attitude was, "It doesn't matter that someone stole my car, because God will get me a better one."

You see, God is able to take what the devil intends for bad and turn it around for good! But if we lose our joy over our circumstances and start griping and complaining, God won't be able to bless us in the midst of that. Instead, we will lose our joy, make ourselves and everyone else around us grumpy, and be frustrated while we sit around and pout.

> **1 THESSALONIANS 1:6**
> **6 And ye became followers of us, and of the Lord, having received the word in much affliction, with joy of the Holy Ghost.**

This verse says that the Word of God was received with much affliction *and* with joy of the Holy Ghost! It's time to let the joy on the inside of your heart flow out into your life — in good times *and* in bad times. It's real easy to let the joy flow during the good times. Anyone can shout when things are going great, but it takes a person with faith in the power of God to keep shouting and praising God when things *aren't* going so good.

Joy in the Kingdom

Romans 14:17 says, *"For the kingdom of God is not meat and drink; but righteousness, and peace, and joy in the Holy Ghost."* In other words, joy in the Holy Ghost is part of the Kingdom of God. And if you're a child of God, you should be taking part in the Kingdom of God. That means you should be experiencing joy in the Holy Ghost!

God is greater than anything — greater than any situation, trial, or circumstance. That's why you can have joy! You have joy because you know how great your God is. And when you know how good your God is, you can be joyful all the time. There's no reason to ever sit around and have a long face. Someone might say, "Well, I had a tough day." It's time to start having *God* days!

When the day starts out tough, turn it over to God!

Too many times, Christians try to do things their own way and in their own strength. They keep all the cares on themselves instead of casting them over to God. When you begin to get bogged down with the cares of the world, remind yourself, *I don't have to care about these problems anymore. I have a greater mentality, and I have Someone else taking care of them now.*

First Peter 5:7 says to cast all of your care on Jesus, because He cares for you. Jesus won't let you down. When you cast your cares on Him, you can live worry-free. Remember, the reason God wants you to live worry-free is so that you can always spend your time rejoicing. But if you are always worried about situations, problems, and circumstances, you can't be joyful. And worry not only affects your physical life, it also affects your prayer life and how much you are able to receive from God.

Joyful Always

People who are filled with the Holy Ghost are joyful and excited *in spite* of what's going on around about them. Of course, problems aren't fun by any means, but they are opportunities to believe God and show that He is bigger than any sickness, poverty, lack, or *any* problem! You can praise Him and be joyful in the midst of anything.

It's time to start living days of heaven upon the earth. Someone might say, "Well, it doesn't feel like heaven where I'm concerned." Then get concerned about something else. If you get full of Holy Ghost joy, then you'll have days of heaven upon the earth in spite of the circumstances around you.

I'm talking about having joy at *all* times — joy when bad news comes, joy when the bills come, joy no matter what the doctor tells you. When trials and bad news come, count it all joy! Let the joy of the Lord be your strength (Neh. 8:10) and begin to rejoice in Him.

Keep Your Tank Full

There is one *infilling* of the Holy Spirit and joy, but there are many *refillings*. Just as you must continually fill your car's gas tank, so you have to keep filling up your spirit with joy in the Holy Ghost. It is better to keep your joy gauge on "full" by continually stirring up the joy that is in you than to have your life run empty of joy.

With a car, if you let your tank level get too low because you let too much time pass between fillings, then you have to pump in a lot more gas in order to fill up your tank. The less fuel you have, the longer it takes you at the gas pump to fill up your tank. But if every time you used some gas, you went to the gas pump and replaced what you used, then your tank would remain full. If you did that, then you would never run out of gas.

The same is true with joy. You can't wait a week or two weeks to refill. Fill up every day, because if you don't fill up every day, it will take you longer to fill up when you need it. When the bills are coming and you have to take an hour to stir up your joy, you're miserable! But if you keep your joy tank full, you can rejoice *always*!

Faith and Joy Go Together

Don't just stir up your joy when you're at church. Stir it up at home! You know there's nothing better than putting the bills on the table and stirring up your joy. It might take a little while to stir it up when you take a look at some of those bills. But keep stirring until you get filled with the joy of the Holy Ghost. The same thing works with your prayer life: Keep praying and believing until you get your answer!

If you put your faith in the power of God, then there's no reason to ever stop believing, because the power of God cannot and will not fail! Don't stop halfway. I've seen people who believed God for six months, and then they stopped. They said, "I guess the answer is not coming."

Then they pouted, cried, and told their friends, "I guess prayer doesn't work. I guess I can't believe God for that."

No, when you're believing God for something, get happy and joyful about it. And then if an obstacle blocks your way and it looks as if you aren't going to receive what you've been believing God for, then get *more* joyful than you were before the obstacle appeared. Of course, you aren't joyful about the obstacle, but about the answer to your prayer. The manifestation of it must be so good that the devil is trying to block it. It must be such a great blessing that he's doing everything he can to stop you from getting hold of it.

Once you put your faith in God's power, don't lean back on what anyone else says. Many times people will tell you things, such as, "You're not going make it. You can't do it. There is no way out." But keep your faith in the power of God and don't listen to what others say, because when there is no way in the natural,

God will make a way! When man says, "You can't do it," God says, "You can do all things through Christ which strengtheneth you" (Phil. 4:13). All things means *all* things — everything. There is no demon in hell and no person on earth who can defeat you. You have the Name of Jesus, and with Jesus on your side, nothing and no one can stop you!

Keep your faith in the power of God. His power will not fail you. Remember that the Greater One is inside you. He is greater than anything you may be facing. So don't stop believing in the power of God. Don't lose your joy. God has your answer! It belongs to you, and it's on the way!